雪天真好玩

The Big Snow

[美]威力·布莱文斯/著　[美]吉姆·帕约/绘

王婧/译

电子工业出版社·

Publishing House of Electronics Industry

北京·BEIJING

Ick and Crud. Book 7, The big snow / by Wiley Blevins; illustrated by Jim Paillot
Copyright © 2019 by Red Chair Press LLC
Published by arrangement with Red Chair Press. All rights reserved.

版权贸易合同登记号　图字：01-2022-0735

图书在版编目（CIP）数据

雪天真好玩 /（美）威力·布莱文斯（Wiley Blevins）著；（美）吉姆·帕约（Jim Paillot）绘；王婧译.
-- 北京：电子工业出版社，2023.6
（胖狗和瘦狗）
ISBN 978-7-121-44941-3

Ⅰ.①雪… Ⅱ.①威… ②吉… ③王… Ⅲ.①儿童故事 – 图画故事 – 美国 – 现代 Ⅳ.①I712.85

中国国家版本馆CIP数据核字(2023)第077353号

责任编辑：范丽鹏
印　　刷：天津图文方嘉印刷有限公司
装　　订：天津图文方嘉印刷有限公司
出版发行：电子工业出版社
　　　　　北京市海淀区万寿路 173 信箱　邮编：100036
开　　本：787×1092　1/16　印张：26.25　字数：264 千字
版　　次：2023 年 6 月第 1 版
印　　次：2023 年 6 月第 1 次印刷
定　　价：208.00 元（全 8 册）

凡所购买电子工业出版社图书有缺损问题，请向购买书店调换。若书店售缺，请与本社发行部联系，联系及邮购电话：(010) 88254888，88258888。
质量投诉请发邮件至 zlts@phei.com.cn，盗版侵权举报请发邮件至 dbqq@phei.com.cn。
本书咨询联系方式：(010) 88254161 转 1862，fanlp@phei.com.cn。

目录

闪亮登场的主角们

克鲁德

艾克

绒球小姐

鲍勃

雪天使

　　"快点儿，"鲍勃打开家门催促着，"'嘘嘘'的时间到了！"

　　克鲁德和艾克从房子里冲了出来。艾克朝着右边跑去，而克鲁德摇摇晃晃地朝着左边走去。他们都在寻找着各自固定"嘘嘘"的地方，可是究竟在哪儿呢？

地上白茫茫的一片，天空中还飘着小雪花。

"用你的舌头接住它们。"克鲁德说。

"接住什么？"艾克问。

"接住那些雪花啊。"克鲁德说。

"接住雪糕？"艾克说，"好吃的！"

"不是，"克鲁德说，"往上看。"

　　艾克歪着脑袋，伸出舌头，郁闷地大叫："我没接住。"

　　"你再试试看。"克鲁德鼓励道。

　　艾克又把舌头伸了出来，一片巨大的雪花落在了他的舌头上。"太棒了！" 艾克开心地叫道，"它竟然是松松脆脆的。我真希望自己是一片雪花啊！"

　　"我也希望自己是一片雪花。"克鲁德说，"又来了一大片哦！"

　　艾克欢快地追着雪花跑来跑去。

3

艾克躺在雪地上，两条左腿往右滑，两条右腿往左滑，四条腿来来回回飞快地在雪地上滑动着。

"瞧啊，"艾克站起来时克鲁德大声喊，"你刚刚做了一个雪天使！"

"哇哦！"艾克开心地笑起来，"那我们再做更多更多的雪天使吧。"

他们在雪地上来来回回滑动着四条腿，做好一个雪天使后便起身换个地方继续玩。没过多久，院子的地上就全是他们做的雪天使了。

"我们是在创作艺术品呢！"艾克说。

"我们做了些东西而已。"克鲁德不太认同。

"是超级美丽的东西。"艾克坚持自己的想法。

"嘿，艾克，"克鲁德叫道，"你现在先别看，有人在盯着我们！"

　　"在哪儿啊？"艾克急忙向四周看去。

　　"她行动起来很轻盈。"克鲁德回答。

　　绒球小姐坐在窗前，像在舔棒棒糖似的轮流舔着自己的两只爪子。她身体稍向前倾，对克鲁德和艾克不屑地哈气。绒球小姐呼出的热气在窗户上留下了一大片雾气，她趁机抬起爪子在上面画了一个大大的"X"。

　　"那是什么意思？"艾克问。

　　克鲁德翻了个白眼儿："我猜应该是她的名字吧。"

　　"哦，"艾克说，"我感觉冷了。"

　　"我也是，"克鲁德说，"我们赶快进屋去吧，哥们儿。"

　　艾克在门前蹭了蹭脚。

　　"我们的脚这会儿都要冻僵啦！"克鲁德汪汪叫起来。

　　"是呀是呀……"艾克呻吟着。

　　"等等，"克鲁德突然想起来什么，"我们忘记去'嘘嘘'啦！"

　　"哦，对啊！"艾克说。

　　这时，鲍勃打开了房门，他抓住克鲁德和艾克的项圈，俩人来不及去"嘘嘘"了。

和鲍勃在一起的欢乐时光

鲍勃蹲在电视机前，克鲁德和艾克待在他身旁。"一场巨大的暴风雪即将来临了，"鲍勃解释着，"看起来我们也许要在家宅上一段时间了。"

克鲁德看着艾克："你知道这是什么意思，对吧？"

"是的，"艾克抬起头，"是什么意思呢？"

"意思就是我们和鲍勃一起愉快玩耍的时间到啦。"克鲁德说。

"哦哦，我最喜欢和鲍勃一起愉快地玩耍啦！"艾克说，"可是我们这次要跟他玩些什么呢？"

"首先，我们和他玩'吓他一跳'的游戏。"克鲁德说。

"好啊好啊，这个好玩。"艾克又问，"那然后呢？"

"然后，我们和他玩儿'躲猫猫'的游戏。"克鲁德回答。

"这个更棒，"艾克说，"我最喜欢躲猫猫的游戏啦！"

“你准备好了吗，哥们儿？”克鲁德问。

“我都听你的。”艾克回答。

说完他们瞪着眼睛跳了起来。克鲁德左右来回地晃着脑袋，而艾克一边转圈一边晃着脑袋。鲍勃这下愣住了。

“你们这是怎么了，小伙子们？”

克鲁德跑到沙发旁，他紧盯着沙发底下，嘴里发出低沉的咆哮声。艾克不停地绕着圈儿跑，一边跑一边尖声汪汪叫着。

嗷

10

　　于是鲍勃蜷缩着趴在地上，慢慢地靠近沙发，朝沙
发底下看了一眼。

　　"这里什么都没有啊，小伙子们！"鲍勃说完抬起
头来，可是克鲁德和艾克早就跑得无影无踪了。

"你们跑哪儿去啦，小伙子们？"鲍勃叫道。

鲍勃一间屋子接着一间屋子地寻找起来，可他既没有看到克鲁德，也没有找到艾克。不过紧接着他发现了窗帘底下露出的一小截来回晃动的小尾巴。

鲍勃踮着脚尖靠近窗帘，"一、二、三……啊哈！"他大叫一声拉开了窗帘。可这里什么也没有。

克鲁德和艾克悄悄地钻到沙发上那张松软毯子的底下。"千万别动，哥们儿！"克鲁德叮嘱道。艾克摇了摇头。

"克鲁德！艾克！"鲍勃大声叫道，"你们在哪儿啊？"他们听到鲍勃的脚步声越来越近了，**踢嗒，踢嗒，踢嗒**。

就在这时，毯子里的一根羽毛忽然落在了艾克的鼻子上。"千万不要动，哥们儿。"克鲁德小声说。然而艾克还是从毯子底下探出头来，甩掉了那根羽毛，又重新钻进毯子底下。可是糟糕，"阿……阿……阿嚏！"这下他可彻底暴露啦！

鲍勃站在他们身旁直摇头，"干得不错呀，小伙子们，"他继续道，"看来你们两个得再去外面溜达溜达了。"

"好的！好的！"克鲁德和艾克开心地叫起来。

邻居的热情款待 3

　　房子外面，雪已经在地上堆积了厚厚的一层，艾克欢快地一头扎进了雪堆里。

　　"你跑哪儿去了，哥们儿？"克鲁德喊道。

　　"在这儿呢，"艾克从雪堆里露出脑袋，"怎么这么冷啊？"

　　"这是雪啊，"克鲁德说，"冰冻凝结之后的水。"

　　"哦，"艾克说，"或许我们到别的地方可以找到一些暖和的雪吧！"

他们和鲍勃一起走出院子，正沿着人行道往前走。这时，一顶蓝帽子突然从围栏另一边冒了出来。

　　"你好啊，鲍勃。"马丁太太打着招呼。

　　"今天可真是一个适合散步的好天气啊。"鲍勃笑着回答。

　　"我刚刚煮了些热巧克力，快进来坐坐吧，我想克鲁德和艾克也需要暖和暖和。"

绒球小姐站在门口。她弓着背，开始哈气，嘴里呼出的热气瞬间变成小冰渣落在她的脚面上。

"哦，不不不不！"克鲁德拒绝道。

"我不要进去，"艾克说，"没门儿，想都别想！"他们扭头便朝人行道跑去。

　　"快点过来啊，小伙子们！别让我把你们抱进去！"鲍勃说着拽住克鲁德的项圈，然后去抓艾克的项圈。但是艾克的动作更快，一眨眼的功夫他就跳进雪堆里，看不见踪影了。

"逮住你啦！"鲍勃大声喊着，他把艾克从雪堆里拽了出来，然后夹在了胳膊底下。

马丁太太站在门口，"我刚刚还烤了些点心招待大家，"她说，"克鲁德和艾克想吃多少都没问题。"

艾克立马从鲍勃胳膊底下跳了出去，克鲁德跳起来翻了个跟头，风风火火地跑进了马丁太太的房子，从叫个没完的绒球小姐旁边擦身而过，径直朝着散发着美味香气的厨房冲了过去。

有只猫在一直盯着我们 4

"这些都是什么呀？"艾克问。

"我从来，哦……哇哦，从来，从来也没有见过这些东西。"克鲁德回答。

他们所见之处全都是猫。猫饼干罐子、猫烤箱隔热手套、猫水杯、猫酒杯、猫毛巾，甚至满墙都是猫爪印儿。

"这里绝对是世界上最可怕的地方。"克鲁德说。

"没错，"艾克说，"没有比这儿更可怕的地方了。"

"也许别的房间没有这么可怕。"克鲁德说。艾克跟着他晃晃悠悠地来到了另一个房间。

然而这间屋子里满眼都是猫枕头、猫窗帘、各式各样猫形状的花盆，甚至连墙纸上的图案也全都是猫。

　　"呃，好恶心。"艾克说。

　　"呃，真恶心，"克鲁德说，"这里简直更可怕！"

　　绒球小姐趴卧在一张小桌子上，长长的尾巴悠闲地晃来晃去。她身下立着一尊金黄色的猫雕像，而雕像旁有一只体形稍小一些的毛茸茸的小猫。

"那是一只真的猫吗？"艾克问。

"我也不知道，哥们儿。"克鲁德说，"那家伙的眼睛眨都不眨一下。"

"可是他们全都在瞪着我们呢……"艾克小声嘟囔着。

克鲁德突然汪汪大叫起来，然而那只小猫依旧一动不动。

"那家伙竟然都没有'喵'一下，"艾克说，"可是它看起来太像一只真的猫了。"

"我也这么觉得。"克鲁德说，"你偷偷地溜过去，然后拍拍它，看看它有什么反应。"

"为什么让我去啊？"艾克表示不满。

"谁让你最小呢。"克鲁德说。

"可是，万一它咬我怎么办？万一它要挠我呢？万一它冲我打喷嚏……我这么小可不能得什么猫身上那些奇怪的病，而且我这么漂亮脸上可不能长出猫的胡须来啊，我这么小……"

"快去吧！"克鲁德催促着，"我帮你打掩护。"

艾克压低了身子，匍匐着向瞪着他们的小猫爬了过去。与此同时，克鲁德两条后腿站起来，一边扭动身子一边汪汪叫着。"你别逗我笑啊……"艾克小声说。

克鲁德用单腿跳跃，并试着跳了一小段吉格舞。可瞪眼的家伙还是一动不动地瞪着他们。

"就快要到啦，"艾克小声说，"不管你刚刚跳的是什么，继续跳啊。"

"我要坚持不住啦！"克鲁德大叫一声。扑通！

24

25

克鲁德朝左滚滚又朝右滚滚，滚来滚去就撞到了艾克的身上。艾克一下被他撞得飞了出去，最后摔在了瞪眼小猫的身上。再然后，小猫又从艾克的身下飞了出去，结果又撞上了那尊金黄色的猫雕像。雕像瞬间翻倒在地，发出"砰"的一声。满地都是金黄色的雕像碎渣渣。

　　"噢，糟糕。"克鲁德说。

　　"噢，不妙。"艾克说。

　　他们拔腿就往门口跑去。马丁太太正站在敞开的大门口。鲍勃跟着他们一同跑出去的时候，还不忘挥手跟马丁太太告别，并大声地说："您把赔偿的账单发给我。"绒球小姐发出一声长长的哈气声，不过听上去却更像是在傻笑。克鲁德和艾克头也不回地朝着人行道冲去，他们穿过雪堆，终于回到了自家的院子。

而且他们赶在鲍勃回来开门之前，找到了各自嘘嘘的好地方。

　　"真高兴我们回家了。"艾克说。

　　"是的，"克鲁德说，"这大雪天里，没有比无猫之家更好的地方啦！"

英文原文

Meet the Characters

Crud

Ick

Miss Puffy

Bob

Snow Angels

"Hurry," said Bob. He opened the door. "It's time for you-know-what."

Ick and Crud raced outside. Ick ran to the right. Crud waddled to the left. Each searched for that just-right spot. But where was it?

雪天使

　　"快点儿，"鲍勃打开家门催促着，"'嘘嘘'的时间到了！"

　　克鲁德和艾克从房子里冲了出来。艾克朝着右边跑去，而克鲁德摇摇晃晃地朝着左边走去。他们都在寻找着各自固定"嘘嘘"的地方，可是究竟在哪儿呢？

1

地上白茫茫的一片，天空中还飘着小雪花。
"用你的舌头接住它们。"克鲁德说。
"接住什么？"艾克问。
"接住那些雪花啊。"克鲁德说。
"接住雪糕？"艾克说，"好吃的！"
"不是，"克鲁德说，"往上看。"

艾克歪着脑袋，伸出舌头，郁闷地大叫："我没接住。"
"你再试试看。"克鲁德鼓励道。
艾克又把舌头伸了出来，一片巨大的雪花落在了他的舌头上。"太棒了！"艾克开心地叫道，"它竟然是松松脆脆的。我真希望自己是一片雪花啊！"
"我也希望自己是一片雪花。"克鲁德说，"又来了一大片哦！"
艾克欢快地追着雪花跑去。

The ground sat covered in a blanket of white. Little flakes fell from the sky.

"Catch them with your tongue," said Crud.

"Catch what?" asked Ick.

"The snowflakes."

"The cupcakes?" asked Ick. "Yum!"

"No," said Crud. "Look up."

Ick tilted his head and stuck out his tongue. "I missed," he cried.

"Try again," said Crud.

Ick stuck out his tongue once more. A big snowflake plopped on it. "Nice!" he said. "It's fluffy and crunchy at the same time. I wish I was a snowflake."

"Me, too," said Crud. "Here comes another big one."

Ick raced to catch it.

艾克躺在雪地上，两条左腿往右滑，两条右腿往左滑，四条腿来来回回飞快地在雪地上滑动着。

"哇啊，"艾克站起来时克鲁德大声喊，"你刚刚做了一个雪天使！"

"嗯哦！"艾克开心地笑起来，"那我们再做更多更多的雪天使吧。"

他们在雪地上来来回回滑动着四条腿，做好一个雪天使后便起身换个地方继续玩。没过多久，院子的地上就全是他们做的雪天使了。

"我们是在创作艺术品呢！"艾克说。

"我们做了些东西而已。"克鲁德不太认同。

"是超级美丽的东西。"艾克坚持自己的想法。

His left feet went right. His right feet went left. He flipped and flapped his legs as fast as he could.

"Look," said Crud, as Ick lifted himself. "You made a snow angel."

"*Ooh!*" said Ick. "Let's make some more."

The two flipped and flopped on the snow. Each flapped his legs. Then they got up and flipped and flopped somewhere else. Before long the yard was filled with doggie snow angels.

"We made art," said Ick.

"We made something," said Crud.

"Something beautiful," whispered Ick.

"Hey, Ick," said Crud. "Don't look now, but someone is watching us."

"Where?" said Ick as he spun to look around.

"Smooth move," said Crud.

Miss Puffy sat in the window. She licked her paws like they were icy lollipops. She leaned in and hissed at them. Her breath made a big foggy spot on the window. Before it could disappear, she lifted her paw and made a big X on it.

"What does that mean?" asked Ick.

Crud rolled his eyes. "I think it's her name."

"Oh," said Ick. "I'm cold."

"Yeah," said Crud. "Let's go in, buddy."

Ick scratched at the front door.

"We're freezing our doggie paws out here!" barked Crud.

"Yeah," moaned Ick.

"Wait," said Crud. "We forgot to do you-know-what."

"Oh, right," said Ick.

Just then Bob opened the door. He grabbed their collars. And it was too late.

2

Playing Fun-with-Bob

Bob squatted in front of the TV. Ick and Crud found spots next to him. "A big storm is coming," he said. "Looks like we might be stuck at home for a while."

Crud look at Ick. "You know what that means, don't you?"

"Yes," said Ick. Then he lifted his head. "What does that mean?"

"It means Fun-with-Bob time," said Crud.

"Oh, I love Fun-with-Bob time," said Ick. "How do we play Fun-with-Bob again?"

"First, we play Scare-Bob."

"Oh, that is fun," said Ick. "Then what?"

"Then we play Hide-from-Bob."

"Yes," said Ick. "That's my favorite."

"你准备好了吗，哥们儿？"克鲁德问。

"我都听你的。"艾克回答。

说完他们瞪着眼睛跳了起来。克鲁德左来右去地晃着脑袋，而艾克一边转圈一边晃着脑袋。鲍勃这下愣住了。

"你们这是怎么了，小伙子们？"

克鲁德跑到沙发旁，他紧盯着沙发底下，嘴里发出低沉的电哮声。艾克不停地绕着圈儿跑，一边跑一边尖声汪叫着。

于是鲍勃蜷缩着趴在地上，慢慢地靠近沙发，朝沙发底下看了一眼。

"这里什么都没有啊，小伙子们！"鲍勃说完抬起头来，可是克鲁德和艾克早就跑得无影无踪了。

"Are you ready, buddy?" asked Crud.

"I will if you will," said Ick.

Both jumped up and stared into the air. Crud twisted his head side to side. Ick twisted and twitched from front to back. Bob shot up.

"What's wrong, boys?"

Crud ran and stared under the couch. He let out a deep growl. Ick ran in circles, yelp-yelp-yelping.

Bob scrunched down. He inched toward the couch. Then slowly he peeked underneath it.

"There's nothing here, boys," said Bob. He lifted his head. But Ick and Crud were nowhere to be seen.

12

13

"Where are you boys?" asked Bob.

Bob went from room to room. No Crud. No Ick. Then he spotted a little tail poking from under a curtain. It wiggled back and forth.

Bob tip-toed to the curtain. "1, 2, 3… A-ha!" he yelled, pushing back the curtain. But nothing was there.

Ick and Crud had slipped underneath the puffy blanket on the couch. "Don't move, buddy," whispered Crud. Ick shook his head.

"Crud! Ick!" yelled Bob. "Where are you?" They could hear his footsteps coming closer. *Clop. Clop. Clop.*

就在这时，毯子里的一根羽毛忽然落在了艾克的鼻子上。"千万不要动，哥们儿。"克鲁德小声说。然而艾克还是从毯子底下探出头来，甩掉了那根羽毛，又重新钻进毯子底下。可是糟糕，"阿……阿……阿嚏！"这下他可彻底暴露啦！

鲍勃站在他们身旁直摇头，"干得不错哟，小伙子们，"他继续道，"看来你们两个得再去外面溜达溜达了。"

"好的！好的！"克鲁德和艾克开心地叫起来。

Just then a feather from the blanket drifted on Ick's nose. "Don't do it, buddy," whispered Crud. Ick poked his head from under the blanket and shook off the feather. Then he slid under the blanket again. But it was too late. Ah-ah-choooo! Off flew the blanket.

Bob stood over them shaking his head. "Nice try, boys," he said. "Maybe you two need to go outside again."

"Yes!" barked Ick and Crud.

Hot Chocolate and Treats

Outside, the snow had quickly piled up. Ick hopped into a big fluffy pile.

"Where are you, buddy?" asked Crud.

"Here," yelled Ick. He poked out his head. "Why is it so cold?"

"It's snow," said Crud. "Frozen water."

"Oh," said Ick. "Maybe we can find warmer snow somewhere else."

邻居的热情款待

房子外面，雪已经在地上堆积了厚厚的一层，艾克欢快地一头扎进了雪堆里。

"你跑哪儿去了，哥们儿？"克鲁德喊道。

"在这儿呢，"艾克从雪堆里露出脑袋，"怎么这么冷啊？"

"这是雪啊，"克鲁德说，"冰冻凝结之后的水。"

"哦，"艾克说，"或许我们到别的地方可以找到一些暖和的雪吧！"

15

39

他们和鲍勃一起走出院子，正沿着人行道往前走。
这时，一顶蓝帽子突然从围栏另一边冒了出来。
"你好啊，鲍勃。"马丁太太打着招呼。
"今天可真是一个适合散步的好天气啊。"鲍勃笑着回答。
"我刚刚煮了些热巧克力，快进来坐坐吧，我想克鲁德和艾克也需要暖和暖和。"

球球小姐站在门口。她弓着背，开始哈气，嘴里呼出的热气瞬间变成小冰渣落在她的脚面上。
"哦，不不不！"克鲁德拒绝道。
"我不要进去，"艾克说，"没门，想都别想！"
他们扭头便朝人行道跑去。

16   17

They headed out of the yard and down the sidewalk with Bob. Just then a big blue hat popped over the fence.

"Hello, Bob," said Mrs. Martin. "Nice day for a walk." Bob laughed.

"I made some fresh hot chocolate. Come on in. I'm sure Ick and Crud would like to warm up."

Miss Puffy stood in the doorway. She arched her back and hissed. Each hiss turned into little bits of ice and fell at her feet.

"Oh, no, no, no," said Crud.

"Not gonna go in there," said Ick. "No way. No how!" They turned and headed back down the sidewalk.

18

"遣住你啦！"鲍勃大声喊着，他把艾克从雪堆里拽了出来，然后夹在了胳膊底下。

马丁太太站在门口，"我刚刚还烤了些点心招待大家，"她说，"克鲁德和艾克想吃多少都没问题。"

艾克立马从鲍勃胳膊底下跳了出去，克鲁德跳起来翻个跟头，风风火火地跑进了马丁太太的房子，从叫个没完的绒球小姐旁边擦身而过，径直朝着散发着美味香气的厨房冲了过去。

"快点过来啊，小伙子们！别让我把你们抱进去！"鲍勃说着拽住克鲁德的项圈，然后去抓艾克的项圈。但是艾克的动作更快，一眨眼的功夫他就跳进雪堆里，看不见踪影了。

19

"Come on, boys. Don't make me carry you in." Bob tugged on Crud's collar. He grabbed at Ick's. But Ick was faster. He jumped into another pile of fluffy snow. And disappeared beneath it.

"Gotcha!" yelled Bob. He pulled out Ick and tucked him under his arm.

Mrs. Martin stood in the doorway. "I have fresh-baked treats, too," she said. "Ick and Crud can have as many as they want!"

Ick leaped out of Bob's arms. Crud jumped up and did a flip. Then the two raced into Mrs. Martin's house, past a hissing Miss Puffy, and straight to the place that smelled so good. The kitchen.

The Cat That Stares

"What is this?" asked Ick.

"I've never… oh-whoa-wow… never, never, never seen anything like it," said Crud.

Everywhere they looked was a cat. A cat cookie jar. Cat oven mitts. Cat cups and glasses. Cat towels. Even cat paw prints on the walls.

"This has to be the worst place on Earth," said Crud.

"Yes," said Ick. "The worst."

"Maybe it'll be better in another room," said Crud. Ick followed as he waddled into the next room.

有只猫在一直盯着我们 4

"这些都是什么呀？"艾克问。

"我从来，哦……哇哦，从来，从来也没有见过这些东西。"克鲁德回答。

他们所见之处全都是猫。猫饼干罐子、猫烤箱隔热手套、猫水杯、猫酒杯、猫毛巾，甚至满墙都是猫爪印儿。

20

"这里绝对是世界上最可怕的地方。"克鲁德说。

"没错，"艾克说，"没有比这儿更可怕的地方了。"

"也许别的房间没有这么可怕，"克鲁德说。艾克跟着他晃晃悠悠地来到了另一个房间。

21

But it was filled with cat pillows. Cat curtains. Cat-shaped flower pots. And cat pictures all over the wall.

"Oh, ick," said Ick.

"Oh, yes," said Crud. "This is even worse!"

Miss Puffy perched on a small table, flipping her tail from side to side. Underneath was a golden cat statue. Beside it was a smaller, furry cat.

"Is it real?" asked Ick.

"I don't know, buddy," said Crud. "Its eyes aren't moving."

"But they're staring right at us," moaned Ick.

Crud barked. The cat didn't move.

"It didn't even meow," said Ick. "But it looks so real."

"I know," said Crud. "You sneak beside it, tap it, and see what happens."

"Why me?" asked Ick.

"You're the smallest," said Crud.

"可是，万一它咬我怎么办？万一它要挠我呢？万一它冲我打喷嚏……我这么小可能得什么猫身上那些奇怪的病，而且我这么漂亮脸上可不能长出猫的胡须来啊，我这么小……"

"快去吧！"克鲁德催促着，"我帮你打掩护。"

艾克压低了身子，匍匐着向瞪着他们的小猫爬了过去。与此同时，克鲁德两条腿站起来，一边扭动身子一边汪汪叫着。"你别逗我笑啊……"艾克小声说。

克鲁德用单腿跳跃，并试着跳了一小段吉格舞。可瞪眼的家伙还是一动不动地瞪着他们。

"就快要到啦，"艾克小声说，"不管你刚刚跳的是什么，继续跳吧。"

"我要坚持不住啦！"克鲁德大叫一声。扑通！

"But what if it bites?" Or scratches? Or sneezes on me? I'm too young to get some weird cat disease. I'm too pretty to grow cat whiskers. I'm too…"

"Just go," said Crud. "I'll distract her."

Ick squatted low to the floor.He wiggled and squiggled toward the cat with the staring eyes. Meanwhile, Crud stood on two legs and barked. He turned and wiggled. "Stop making me laugh," whispered Ick.

Then Crud hopped on one leg and tried to dance a little jig. The cat just stared and stared.

"Almost there," whispered Ick. "Keep dancing, or whatever you call that."

"I… I… I can't," yelled Crud. Plop!

26

克鲁德朝左滚滚又朝右滚滚，滚来滚去就撞到了艾克的身上。艾克一下被他撞得飞了出去，最后摔在了瞪眼小猫的身上。再然后，小猫又从艾克的身下飞了出去，结果又撞上了那尊金黄色的猫雕像。雕像瞬间翻倒在地，发出"砰"的一声。满地都是金黄色的雕像碎渣渣。

"噢，糟糕。"克鲁德说。

"噢，不妙。"艾克说。

他们拔腿就往门口跑去。马丁太太正站在敞开的大门口。鲍勃跟着他们一同跑出去的时候，还不忘挥手跟马丁太太告别，并大声地说："您把赔偿的账单发给我。"绒球小姐发出一声长长的哈气声，不过听上去却更像是在傻笑。克鲁德和艾克头也不回地朝着人行道冲去，他们穿过雪堆，终于回到了自家的院子。

27

Crud rolled left. Then he rolled right. He rolled and rolled until he rolled into Ick. Ick flipped and landed on top of the staring cat. The cat flew from under him and hit the golden cat statue. It toppled over and CRASH! Tiny golden cat pieces scattered everywhere.·

"Oh, crud," said Crud.

"Oh, no," said Ick.

The two raced to the front door. Mrs. Martin stood there with the door already open. Bob followed them out. "Send me the bill," he shouted as he waved goodbye. Miss Puffy let out a long hiss that sounded more like a giggle. Ick and Crud sped down the sidewalk, through the piles of snow, and into their yard.

而且他们赶在鲍勃回来开门之前，找到了各自嘘嘘的好地方。

"真高兴我们回家了。"艾克说。

"是的，"克鲁德说，"这大雪天里，没有比无猫之家更好的地方啦！"

28

And just before Bob could open the door, they both found the perfect spot for you-know-what.

"I'm sure glad we're home," said Ick.

"Yes," said Crud. "There's no better place to be than a cat-free home on a snowy day!"